ook at
awrence

like
similar

1.Biology—Classification I.Title

# Like and Unlike

## A First Look at Classification

BY SOLVEIG PAULSON RUSSELL

ILLUSTRATED BY LAWRENCE DI FIORI

HENRY Z. WALCK, INC.          NEW YORK

Text copyright © 1973 by Solveig Paulson Russell
Illustrations copyright © 1973 by Lawrence Di Fiori
All rights reserved
ISBN: 0-8098-1209-6
LC: 73-4647
Printed in the United States of America

Library of Congress Cataloging in Publication Data
Russell, Solveig Paulson. Like and unlike.
SUMMARY: Describes the grouping of alike things,
or classification of similar objects, with emphasis
on plants and animals.
1. Classification of sciences—Juvenile literature.
[1. Biology—Classification. 2. Classification of sciences.]
I. Di Fiori, Lawrence, illus. II. Title.
Q177.R87        574'.01'2        73-4647
ISBN 0-8098-1209-6

*To all young people whose interests lead them*
*through the open door of scientific investigation*

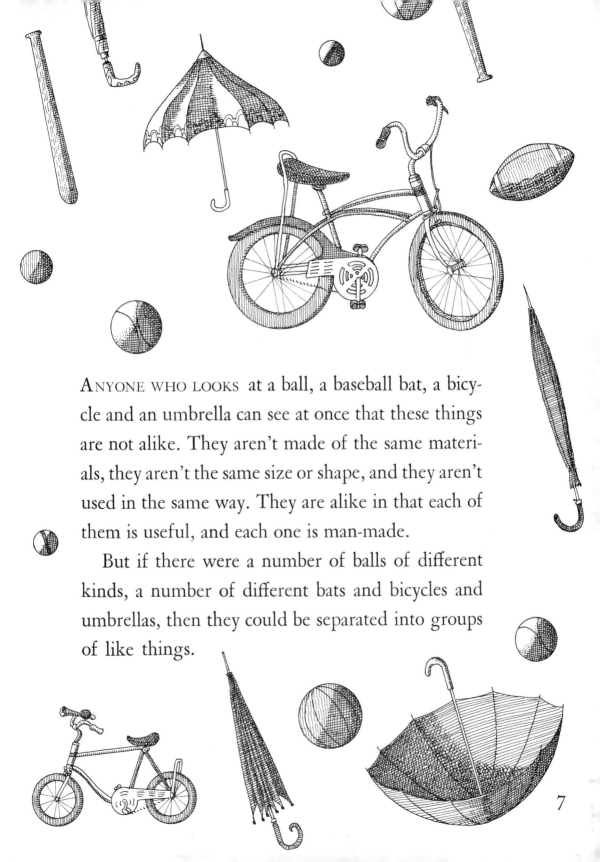

ANYONE WHO LOOKS at a ball, a baseball bat, a bicycle and an umbrella can see at once that these things are not alike. They aren't made of the same materials, they aren't the same size or shape, and they aren't used in the same way. They are alike in that each of them is useful, and each one is man-made.

But if there were a number of balls of different kinds, a number of different bats and bicycles and umbrellas, then they could be separated into groups of like things.

7

First, all of the balls would go in one large group, the bats would go in another, the bicycles would make up a third group, and the umbrellas would make a fourth group, or set.

Then we would see that all the balls were not exactly alike. We could sort them according to what game they would be used in. We could put the baseballs in one group, and the footballs, the basketballs, the tennis balls, the croquet balls, the balls for playing jacks in separate groups. We might have five or six groups of different kinds of balls.

In each of these groups there would be differences, too. Some balls would be new, some old, some dirty, some colored, some might have names on them. Every difference would make it possible to separate the group into smaller sets.

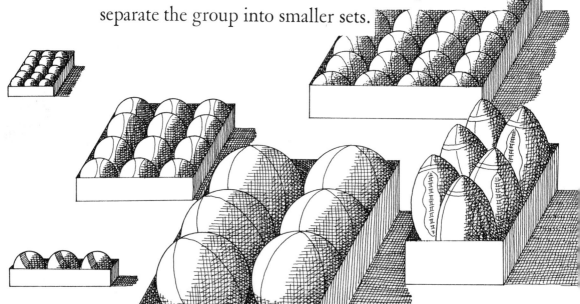

The baseball bats could be sorted by size, by color, by weight and by what they were made of. The bicycles could be separated into a girls' group and a boys' group. These two main divisions could be divided again several times, into sets according to number of speeds, types of seats and handlebars, colors, and so on. The umbrellas could be big, little, men's or women's. They could be sorted by colors, by materials, by the way the handles were made, by the number of ribs each had, or by the country where they were made.

Sorting into like groups makes for order, and order makes life easier in a number of ways. If this were not so you can imagine what a mess there would be in a department store, for example, that had no orderly way of sorting the things it wished to sell. Hats would sit on garbage cans, shoes might be on washing machines, pets would have a grand time with groceries, and there would be no end to confusion.

Making order from a large number of different objects requires that the person putting them into groups needs to note the ways the things are alike and the ways they differ.

All over the world, every bit of knowledge of everything can be sorted in many different ways. Putting things that are alike together gives us order. Then we can better understand and see how things work, or are related, and know where to find them.

SORTING LIVING THINGS

When scientists sort or group living things—plants and animals—they use the word classification. Every group classified includes living things that are alike in some way. Classification is a sorting-out of likenesses.

From very early times people have given special names to plants and animals. Aristotle, a Greek who lived over 2,000 years ago, was the first known man to carefully study them. He gave names to over five hundred plants and five hundred animals. Then a Roman named Pliny, who lived two hundred years later than Aristotle, added more knowledge to the study of living things. But knowledge about them grew slowly for a long time.

The man best known for his work in classification, and who perhaps deserves the most credit for beginning the modern ways of sorting living things, was Carolus Linnaeus. He was born in Sweden in 1707, and died in 1778.

As a young child, Carolus was unusually interested in flowers and plants. His father taught him all he knew about them, but the boy wanted to know more. As he grew he constantly studied living things, and when he was in the university he spent his summers studying plants and animals in Lapland. He wanted to be able to arrange collections of things in an orderly way.

When he graduated from the university, Linnaeus published a book he had written called *The System of Nature*. It described the ways he had invented for classifying plants and animals. Scientists everywhere quickly accepted his plan, and it is still used all over the world as a basic plan.

In the last two hundred years scientists have been improving methods of classification and they are still doing so. Each year a great number of new living things are discovered, many of them exceedingly small. As they are discovered, scientists try to find out where they belong in the classification systems of plants and animals. Sometimes changes have to be made in old systems to take care of new discoveries.

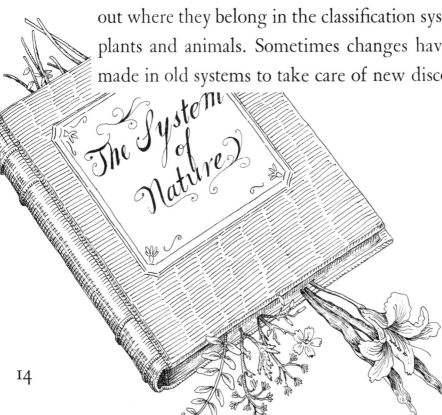

*Dolichonyx oryzivorus!!*

## LINNAEUS'S PLAN

In his plan for classifying plants and animals, Linnaeus invented a name-language. Each plant and animal was given two names, both Latin. These are known as the "scientific" names.

Linnaeus chose Latin names for classification because Latin was a language known to many educated people in all parts of the world when he wrote his book. Latin words meant exactly the same thing to everyone who used them. Thus an Englishman, a Turk, a German, a Swiss, or any scientist anywhere would not be confused. They all knew that the same Latin word meant the same thing. The Latin names are still used today.

*Bobolink!*

Common names, unlike Latin ones, are not the same everywhere. Bobolink is a common name for a bird that, in different parts of our country, is often called a redbird or ricebird. If someone didn't know this, he would think they were three different birds. When the Latin or scientific name—*Dolichonyx oryzivorus*—is used, it shows that only one kind of bird is being spoken of.

The flicker is also known as a golden-winged woodpecker, a high-hole or a yellow-hammer. The flicker's scientific name would tell you they are all the same bird. The plant ragweed is called Roman wormwood, bitter-weed, wild tansy, hayweed, bog-weed, carrotwood and stammer-wart. These are common names for one plant. The word gopher means a squirrel-like animal to some people. To others a gopher is a land turtle. The scientific names would show that they are two different animals.

## CLASSIFICATION ACCORDING TO STRUCTURE

When anyone studies plants or animals to try to classify them, he has to look carefully to decide how they are made—how the different parts are put together in different ways. He looks at many plants or animals and notices the ways they are alike. He compares them for likenesses or differences so that he can separate them into groups, or sets. If he is studying leaves, he sees if the ends are blunt or pointed, or have bristles on them. He sees whether the tiny veins in them branch out or run straight, and he notices the color and thickness of each. He may study the stem and blossoms, seeds and fruit.

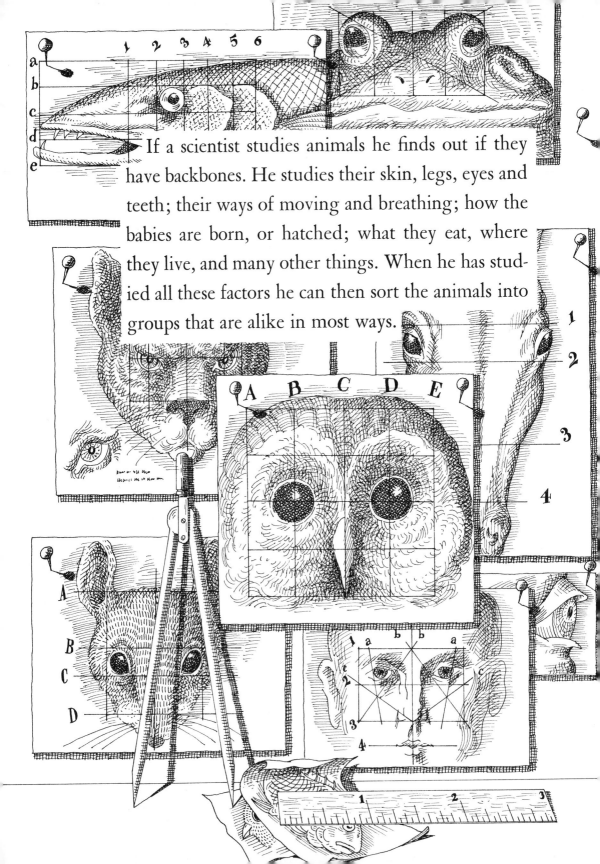

If a scientist studies animals he finds out if they have backbones. He studies their skin, legs, eyes and teeth; their ways of moving and breathing; how the babies are born, or hatched; what they eat, where they live, and many other things. When he has studied all these factors he can then sort the animals into groups that are alike in most ways.

SCIENTIFIC CLASSIFICATION OF PLANTS AND ANIMALS

Scientists classify plants and animals in the following order, beginning with the largest grouping, and working downward to smaller groups.

*Kingdom*

You may have played the question game where one person thinks of some object to be guessed, and the other players see if they can guess what it is with not more than twenty questions. To start the game somebody usually asks, "Is it animal, vegetable, or mineral?"

Everything in nature fits into one of these kingdoms. Animals include all living things that are not plants. Vegetable includes all plants. Minerals include all non-living parts of earth.

These three groups are sometimes called the three "kingdoms" of earth. They are huge groups and each has many smaller sub-groups under it. For example, the animal kingdom includes people, birds, fish, four-footed animals, insects, snakes, lizards,

frogs and toads. The plant kingdom includes all kinds of plants—some so tiny they can't be seen without a microscope. Minerals, such as water and rocks, are not living and have never been alive.

In nature everything can be grouped or sorted as living or non-living things. Scientists speak of all living things as organisms. Organisms are all the plants and animals. Living organisms are always made of material which can replace parts of itself when needed, and living organisms can move by them-

selves. If you skin your knee you will soon have new skin where the old skin was lost. Cut hair grows again. When a crab loses a claw he grows another claw to replace the lost one. Plants turn as they grow to face the light. Living things change, or grow all the time. And all living things can make new ones like themselves, or reproduce.

Non-living things cannot reproduce, and they can't grow. They can't move by themselves, breathe or feel.

# Phylum Protozoa

# Phylum Annelida

# Phylum Arthropoda

*Phylum*

The plant and animal kingdoms are both made of divisions called *phyla*. *Phylum* is the word for only one of these divisions; *phyla* means more than one.

There are many phyla for large groups of animals. Animals made of only one cell belong to Phylum *Protozoa*. The earthworm, which has a body made up of separate sections, or segments, belongs to Phylum *Annelida*. In the Phylum *Arthropoda* all the members have jointed legs, antennae, hard outside skeletons, and three regions of body. Another phylum, *Chordata,* includes animals with backbones—dogs, cats, horses, deer, fish, birds and others, including ourselves. There are many times more animals without backbones than there are with backbones.

**Phylum Chordata**

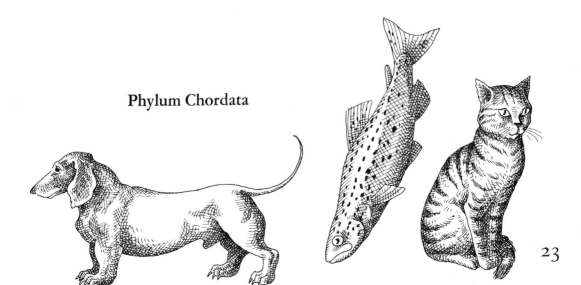

23

*Class*

Classes are the next smaller division. Each of the phyla is made up of several classes. For example, the phylum of animals that have backbones is divided into the classes of fish, amphibians, reptiles, birds and mammals.

Fish live in water. They can move about in it, and get oxygen through their gills. Amphibians are those creatures that begin life in water and change so that they can live on land. They breathe first through gills, and later through lungs. They include the frogs, toads, newts and salamanders. Reptiles are the snakes, crocodiles, alligators, turtles and lizards. Reptiles have scales or bony plates on their skin. They breathe with lungs, and so, even though some of them go into the water, they must come up for air. Birds are the only animals with feathers.

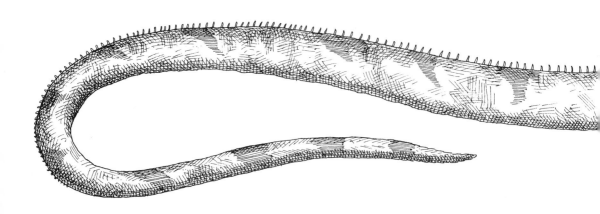

The animals classed as mammals all have warm blood, and the females have milk to feed their young. Their body cavities are divided into two parts—one for heart and lungs, and one for stomach and intestines. All have hair on their bodies. Many people think all mammals give birth to live babies, but there are a few—like the platypus—that do lay eggs.

A dog belongs to the mammal class. A frog is classed as an amphibian.

*Order*

The order is the next lower classification after classes in sorting living things.

Different animals have characteristics that affect, or determine their ways of life. Some birds have heavy thick claws, or talons, for grabbing and holding the creatures they eat. These are the hawks and eagles. Birds that wade in water need long legs, such as those of the stork and the heron. The birds that live in water part of the time, the ducks and geese, for example, have paddling feet with web between the toes. Some birds, such as chickens and quail, live on the ground, scratching for food in the dirt.

The bird class is divided into order groups based on their differences. There is the order of perching birds, the order of birds of prey, the order of woodpeckers, and others.

In the class of mammals, some orders are those of the meat-eaters, the hoofed animals, and the gnawing, or chewing animals. In the reptile class, reptiles that don't have ears or eyelids are grouped into the order of serpents (snakes).

Dogs are in the order of meat-eaters. Frogs belong in the order called anura.

Each living thing belongs in only one order. It may seem that some creatures belong in two or more orders. You may think that the order of meat-eaters should include eagles because eagles eat meat. You may think that a shark should be in the order of meat-eaters too. But an eagle is a bird, a creature with feathers, and a shark is a fish, a creature with scales covering his body. Though these two do eat meat, they are not put into the same order because they have more differences than likenesses. Each creature is in any group because he has likenesses in common with other creatures in this group—likenesses not found in creatures outside the group.

*Family*

    In a family all the members resemble each other closely in the ways they are made. One family of the bird class and the order of fowl-like birds includes the chicken, quail, peacock, turkey, and pheasant. All of these birds have feet that are made alike. Their heads, necks and bodies are built in the same way. None of them have webbed feet or very long necks as some other birds of a different family have.

The cat family, *Felidae,* (class of mammals, order of meat-eaters) includes the cat, mountain lion, tiger, leopard, wild cat, puma and other "big cats." The bodies of all of these are made in the same way.

The *Acride* family, of the class of insects and the order of straight wings, is the family of locusts or grasshoppers. All the members of this family have hind legs that are stronger and longer than their middle pair of legs.

The rose family, of the class of *Dicotyledons,* and the order of *Rosales*, is very large. It includes not only roses, but also apple, plum, strawberry, raspberry and other plants, all of which have flowers and fruit that resemble those of the rose.

Each order of plants or animals is made up of many of these different families. As the classifying groups grow smaller, the animals and plants in each are more closely related, or more alike.

*Genus*

As we have said, Linnaeus gave two names to living things. The first part of the name is the genus name. The word for more than one genus is *genera*. Genera are sub-divisions of the family.

In the cat family, cats, leopards, cougars, lions and tigers are much alike. They are put together in the genus grouping called *Felis,* meaning cat in Latin. They are all made in the same way and their actions are similar. They hunt by stalking for food, and they most often hunt alone.

The dog family includes, among others, dogs, wolves and coyotes. *Canis* is the name for the genus group of these animals. Dogs, wolves and coyotes are similar in their bodies. They move alike, and hunt in packs.

*Species*

The second part of scientific names for living things tells the *species* to which they belong. Species is a smaller classification group than is a genus group. Each genus may be made up of many different species of plants or animals. An example of this is that in Eastern North America there are five species of thrushes: the wood thrush, the hermit thrush, the olive-backed thrush, the gray-cheeked thrush and the veery.

Each species in any genus can only breed with its own kind and cannot reproduce with other kinds in other families. Thus robins always have baby robins, and bluebirds always have baby bluebirds.

In the cat genus there are individuals that differ in size and other characteristics, so they are divided into species with names to show these divisions. The cat is *Felis domestica,* the cougar is *Felis cougar,* and the lion is *Felis leo.*

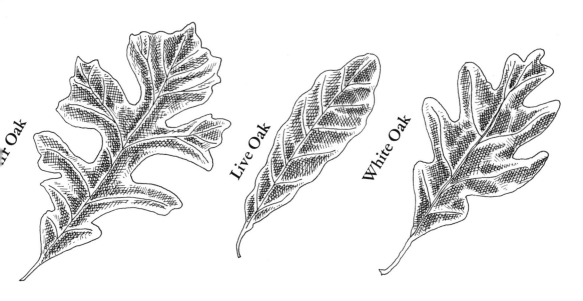

The dog has the genus name *Canis familiaris. Familiaris* is the species part of this name. The wolf is *Canis lupus* and the coyote is *Canis latrans.*

All oak trees belong to the genus with the Latin name of *Quercus.* But there are several kinds of oak trees—the live oak, the pin oak, the white oak, the burr oak and others. These differ in size, leaf shapes, acorns and other ways. Each of these oaks is a species of oak and so each also has a Latin species name. The white oak is *Quercus alba,* and the red oak is *Quercus borealis.*

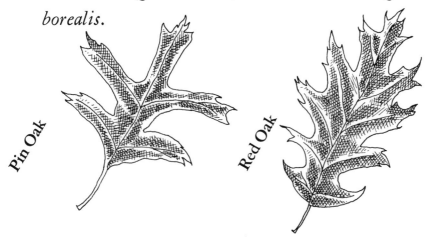

When we write these names we always write a genus name with a capital letter, but use a small letter for a species name. Groups larger than species—phyla, classes, orders, families—have one name only, but species always have a two-part name made up of the genus and another name which sets it apart from other species in the same genus. This is like having a human Smith group, with names of Smith Mary, Smith John, and Smith Ellen.

The species names may describe something about the species. The species names of *Xanthoxylum* (yellow wood) and *Cerocarpus* (coiled fruit) tell something in Latin about these plants. Some names come from those used by ancient people, such as the old Greek names of *Quercus, Fagus* and *Betula* for oak, beech and birch trees. Names may also honor a person. Examples of this are *Jeffersonia* for Thomas Jefferson, *Linnaea* for Linnaes, and *Louisia* for Captain Merriwether Lewis, an explorer.

The species part of the scientific names usually describes something about a plant or animal, or refers to the place where it was discovered. *Rosa alba* is a white rose; *Ulmus americana* is the American elm.

*Varieties*

You may have heard of varieties of things. When scientists use this word in classifying, variety tells the name of a thing which has a slight difference from other things in its species. But the difference is not enough to class it as a separate species. Sometimes varieties are called sub-species. Sub-species can breed or reproduce with other members of the same species.

Today classifying by variety is not used as often as it once was. It sometimes led to confusion when plants or animals from different areas showed slight differences due to their environment.

However in plant catalogs plants are still often spoken of as being of a certain variety. Apple trees are good examples of this. Apple trees are a species of fruit tree with the Latin name of *Pyrus malus,* but

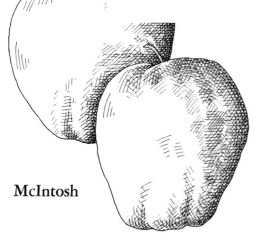

McIntosh

Rome

there are apples with the common names such as Northern Spies, Baldwins, Jonathans, and others that have slight differences. These are *varieties* of apples.

The differences are in such things as whether the apples stay firm a long time and so will last into winter, or whether they are best in the fall. All apples are rounded in shape, but some varieties have small bumps at the base, such as the Delicious variety has. Some varieties are yellow, some red, some streaked with color. These varieties are not given Latin names because, like dogs and domestic cats, they have been bred by man for special reasons and would not be found by themselves in nature.

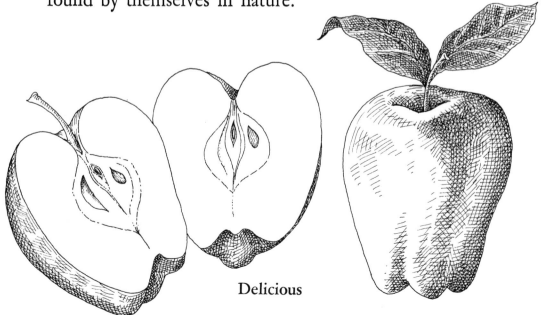

Delicious

Looking back we see that the scheme scientists use to classify plants and animals is 1. Kingdom 2. Phylum 3. Class 4. Order 5. Family 6. Genus 7. Species and, sometimes, 8. Variety. This arrangement starts from the largest grouping and works down to the smaller ones.

If we followed the scientist's way for classifying people, using the classifications we have just listed, we could find that people everywhere are of

1) The animal kingdom
2) The phylum *Chordata* (animals with backbones)
3) The class of *Mammalia* (having hair or fur, warm blood, milk from mothers, etc.)
4) The order of *Primates* (monkeys, apes, and man—use fingers and brains well)

5) Family of *Hominidae* (all manlike creatures who ever walked on hind legs)

6) The genus of *Homo* (manlike animal)

7) The species of *Sapiens* (the wise—having wisdom)

OTHER CLASSIFICATIONS

Classification, as we have seen, is used for order and understanding. All things can be classified, and classifications are important everywhere.

Ecology is the study of how living things affect, and are affected by their surroundings. Ecology students classify the world into large areas called *realms*.

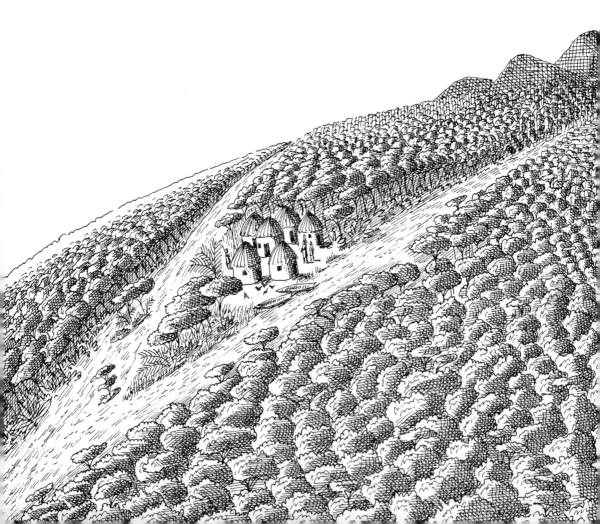

Then they divide these large parts of earth into smaller divisions known as *biomes* which have special kinds of climate. The biomes are divided into smaller areas known as *habitats* where the surroundings are right for certain living things. The smallest division in ecology is the *niche,* the home of an animal or plant.

A system of classification used by millions of people each day is the classification of books in libraries. Without the grouping together of books about the same subjects, libraries would be almost useless for people looking for information.

Food, too, is classified. All food can be classified into the nourishment groups of *proteins, carbohydrates, fats, vitamins* and *minerals*.

Classifying is a part of life. Everyone classifies. Anyone who has a stamp, coin or shell collection, or a collection of any kind, sorts out and groups the different things he has. Even when we make lists, or when we just think about objects or activities and how they are related, we are classifying. Without this orderly way of putting like things together our world would be a topsy-turvy place indeed.

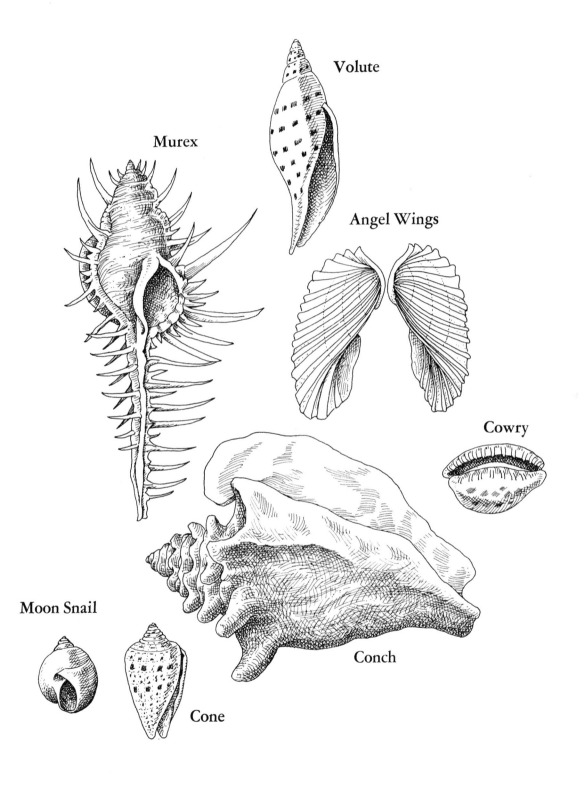

Volute

Murex

Angel Wings

Cowry

Moon Snail

Cone

Conch